SHELBY

Steve Statham

First published in 1996 by Motorbooks International Publishers & Wholesalers, 729 Prospect Avenue, PO Box 1, Osceola, WI 54020-0001 USA

© Steve Statham, 1996

All rights reserved. With the exception of quoting brief passages for the purpose of review no part of this publication may be reproduced without prior written permission from the Publisher

Motorbooks International is a certified trademark, registered with the United States Patent Office

The information in this book is true and complete to the best of our knowledge. All recommendations are made without any guarantee on the part of the author or Publisher, who also disclaim any liability incurred in connection with the use of this data or specific details

We recognize that some words, model names and designations, for example, mentioned herein are the property of the trademark holder. We use them for identification purposes only. This is not an official publication

Motorbooks International books are also available at discounts in bulk quantity for industrial or sales-promotional use. For details write to Special Sales Manager at the Publisher's address

Library of Congress Cataloging-in-Publication Data Available

Statham, Steve
    Shelby / Steve Statham.
      p. cm. -- (Motorbooks International enthusiast color series)
    Includes index.
    ISBN 0-7603-0124-7 (pbk. : alk. paper)
    1. Shelby automobile--History. I. Title.
    II. Series: Enthusiast color series.
    TL215.S48S73   1996
    629.222'2--dc20   95-50782

On the front cover: This 1967 GT500 is owned by Tom Daniel

On the frontispiece: A row of Daytona Coupes.

On the title page: A Shelby Mustang GT500KR "King of the Road" rests in front of a North American T-6.

On the back cover: This 427 Cobra is one of the first fifty-two 427 Cobras built, and was invoiced as an S/C with full factory competition prep.

Printed in Hong Kong

CONTENTS

Acknowledgments
6

ONE
Cobras and Glory
9

TWO
Mustangs Get Help
35

THREE
Dodge Days
73

Index
96

Acknowledgments

When it comes to putting a project like this book together, there are always plenty of people who deserve honest thanks and heartfelt gratitude.

To start, I'd like to thank all those who took time from their busy schedules for interviews, including Pete Brock, Bill Neale, and Tim Pettijohn. Thanks, gentlemen, for providing new insights as well as patiently rehashing old news. Also on the receiving end of my gratitude are those who contributed crucial photography to this book, individuals such as Dave Friedman and Mike Mueller, as well as Donald Farr and Greg Rager of Dobbs Publishing and Brandt Rosenbusch of Chrysler Historical.

Most of the production numbers used in this book came from the acknowledged source of Shelby trivia, the Shelby American Auto Club's 1987 World Registry. Other valuable reference sources include Dave Friedman and John Christy's Carroll Shelby's *Racing Cobra*, and Carroll Shelby's 1967 autobiography (with John Bentley) *The Carroll Shelby Story*. Ray Christ at the Shelby Dodge Automobile Club deserves thanks for making my weekend with his club members informative, easy-going, and fun.

Certainly, I thank those car owners who allowed me to photograph their cars for use in this book. In my coast-to-coast travels I met many enthusiastic Shelby owners, and whether Cobra or Omni fans, all were unfailingly helpful and good-natured. These good people include:

Tom Daniel, DeSoto, Texas, 1967 GT500; Gary Bennett and Jim Philion, Tulsa, Oklahoma, 427 Competition Cobra; Curtis D. Burton, Houston, Texas, 1968 GT500KR convertible; Harris Conner, Chamblee, Georgia, 1965 GT350R; Greg Hillman, Dallas, Texas, 1969 GT500; Tim Hoover, Hollidaysburg, Pennsylvania, 1988 CSX-T; Jim Edick, North Syracuse, New York, 1989 Shelby Dakota; Rick Ehrmann, Landover, Maryland, 1987 Shelby Lancer; David Loebenberg, St. Petersburg, Florida, 1967 GT500 Super Snake; Bob Lowry, Golden, Colorado, 1970 GT350 convertible; Bill McPeak, De Land, Florida, 1986 Omni GLHS; Bill Neal, Houston, Texas, 1965 GT350; Sean Ogara, Brooklyn Center, Minnesota, 1987 Charger GLHS; Greg Rager, Lakeland, Florida, 1991 Daytona Shelby IROC; Kevin Rich, Pflugerville, Texas, 1966 GT350H and 1967 Trans-Am Mustang; Drew Serb, Moraga, California, 289 Cobra and Competition Prep 427 Cobra; Denny Shaw, Duncansville, Pennsylvania, 1986 Shelby Charger; Michael Shoen, Phoenix, Arizona, Cobra Daytona Coupe.

Finally, every red-blooded car enthusiast has to thank Carroll Shelby for creating so many fast, fun, and exhilarating cars. A few seconds behind the wheel of a 289 Cobra was all it took to make me completely understand why so many people live, eat, and breathe Shelby automobiles. Here's hoping the enthusiasm never wanes.

ONE

Cobras And Glory

The thing in life that spells "success" is to take advantage of the right opportunity.
—Carroll Shelby, The Carroll Shelby Story

In Carroll Shelby's long and remarkable career, this philosophy—taking advantage of opportunities—is one Shelby has had little trouble sticking to. As a chicken farmer, pilot, race car driver, driving school owner, car dealer, Goodyear tire distributor, sports car manufacturer, and chili maven, Shelby has indeed taken advantage of innumerable opportunities, his great successes offsetting his few failures.

The opportunity Carroll Shelby is most remembered for is dropping Ford's lightweight, small-block V-8 into an English roadster and creating a fun, affordable, and ferocious sports car—Shelby's Cobra.

At a time when the idea of starting a car company was about the quickest way to get laughed out of town, it is remarkable that Shelby was able to put the whole enterprise together. But by playing on his success as a race car driver, his considerable entrepreneurial skills and his dogged determination, Shelby

Interior of the very first Cobra, CSX2000, owned by Carroll Shelby since new. The early Cobras had side curtains rather than roll-up windows, a primitive top, cramped footwells, and little insulation from engine heat, but who cared? The car was supposed to be fun, and fun meant speed, not comfort.

The very first Cobras kept the AC designation, which was dropped on later models. Subsequent Cobras were badged with an illustrated Cobra emblem and "Powered by Ford" emblems on the cars' fenders.

was able to do what was considered impossible: he created his own sports car company.

Born in 1923 in Leesburg, Texas, Shelby developed an interest in cars and aviation at an early age. He first scratched the aviation itch while serving more than four years in the Army Air Corps flying and then training future bomber pilots. After he left the army in 1945, Shelby attempted a number of minor business ventures before establishing a career as a race car driver. Sports car racing, while fun, was not a lucrative career in those days, and there were some years when it didn't pay at all. Shelby spent many years in the early fifties as a racing vagabond, traveling from hotel to race track and back, surviving on assorted minor business deals.

With perseverance and backing from people like John Edgar and John Wyer, racing began to pay off. Shelby became a nationally known driver in the late fifties when his sports car racing success landed him on the cover of *Sports Illustrated*, which named him Driver of the Year for both 1956 and 1957. He was the colorful Texan who raced in striped bib

Dave MacDonald, shown driving a 289 Cobra at Del Mar in 1963. MacDonald was part of an incredibly talented group of men who drove for Shelby, including Ken Miles, Dan Gurney, Phil Hill, and Bob Holbert. MacDonald was later killed in a crash at the 1964 Indianapolis 500. *Dave Friedman Photo Collection*

After the first 75 Cobras were sold with the 260ci engine, the 289ci-engined models came on line. A total of 580 289 Cobras were built, more than any other Cobra model.

overalls driving Maseratis, Porsches, Alfa Romeos, and Aston Martins—all the great sports cars of the time.

As the winner of three national sports car championships in the fifties and the 1959 24 Hours of Le Mans, Shelby established a reputation as one of the best race car drivers of his time. He was also well known as a unique individual. "The thing that struck me, he was, and still is, one of the calmest people in a race car I have ever seen," recalled long-time Shelby friend Bill Neale. "He also—unlike some drivers—would,

The standard 289ci Cobra engine came with a four-barrel carburetor, but the four downdraft Weber set-up was available as an option. Also available through Shelby's performance catalog were dual four-barrel and three two-barrel induction systems. In the 1960s, Weber systems like this were advertised by Ford for $695, no small sum today but a fortune at the time.

without bothering or irritating the car owner or mechanic, really look over everything. He really had a good eye for looking at the stuff. He just didn't go crawl in and drive."

Neale also recalls Shelby's relaxed attitude before races. "About thirty minutes before a race, or close to that, he'd find a car, some four-door sedan if possible. He'd open the two back doors and lay down in that thing and take a nap. I watched him do that many times around a race track, and he'd say, 'Wake me up when it's time to grid.'"

Even while enjoying his racing success, Shelby was looking ahead. "Except at the very beginning, I never considered motor racing as an end in itself, but only as a means to something bigger, more important, and more permanent," he recalled in his 1967 autobiography. Although at the time he wasn't sure just what those bigger, more important things would be, the racing experience helped narrow his focus.

"The longer I went on racing and was around the limited-production factories in Europe, the more I realized that America was missing a big bet, a winning bet, and that it was time someone responsible got their eyes open," Shelby relays in *The Carroll Shelby Story*. "To put it briefly, that winning bet I'm talking about was the design and production of an all-purpose, all-American sports or grand touring car that you could drive to market and also race during the weekend, without having to spend $15,000 to $17,000 dollars or go into hock for the rest of your life, only to own an automobile which, next year, might be out of date technically." This fairly well sums up Shelby's life-long philosophy of auto production.

After heart problems forced Shelby to retire from auto racing in 1960, he found himself with a lot more time to work on implementing that philosophy. He opened his Shelby School of High Performance Driving and worked as a Goodyear tire distributor after his retirement but also continued working on his dream to build an American sports car.

In September of 1961, Shelby hit on the right combination. Upon hearing that AC cars of England had lost the Bristol Aeroplane Company as an engine supplier and consequently was likely to cease production of its Ace sports car, Carroll quickly contacted AC and presented his idea of a European-type sports car with an American engine. AC management was receptive to the idea, so Shelby zeroed in on an engine supplier. He had kicked around the idea of using Chevrolet or Buick engines, but it was Ford that both showed the most interest and had the right type of powerplant—a new, lightweight small-block 221ci V-8 engine.

While preliminary work was beginning on a Shelby prototype, Ford increased the displacement of the new engine

By the time 1964 models like this one were in production, the Cobras had incorporated six-inch wire-spoke wheels, side vent windows, and an alternator in place of the earlier cars' generator. The rear differential gear ratio had by then been switched from 3.54:1 to 3.77:1. The roll bar was a competition option.

to 260ci, and Shelby's people found ways to pump the horsepower level to 260 at 5800 rpm. Soon after, Shelby had one of the engines shipped to England. He then flew over to guide development.

What Shelby found was that the 260ci engine and Ford four-speed transmission fit in the car well enough, but most other chassis and drivetrain components on the AC Ace were not able to handle American V-8 levels of horsepower. To make an Ace a Shelby, Carroll specified a larger Salisbury rear end assembly with 3.54:1 axle ratio, a sturdier front suspension, four-wheel Girling disc brakes, chassis reinforcements, and an altered body with slightly flared fenders. The car was named Cobra, a name that Shelby says came to him in a dream.

The Cobra was much more than just an Ace with an engine swap. "If they think there's not a lot of difference between an Ace Bristol and a Cobra, all I'd ask them to do is go drive one of those damned old Ace Bristols. I mean, it rattled and shook, and didn't have enough power to pull your hat off," Bill Neale says to non-believers, if any still exist.

With the bugs more or less worked out, the first car was completed in February, 1962, and shipped back to California, where the serious work of setting up production began. Ford offered engines on credit and lent some engineering support while AC built the chassis to Shelby's specifications and shipped them to Shelby's facilities for completion. The price was set at $5,995. The first car was sold in mid-1962, and the Cobra legend was off and running.

Things started with a bang. The second car built was the first to be raced. Cobra's competitive debut was at Riverside in October 1962, and driver Bill Krause led the race until a broken wheel hub sidelined the car, allowing a Corvette to win. But victories soon followed in SCCA Regional events and USRRC races. By the end of the 1963 season, Cobras had won the USRRC Manufacturers' Championship, and Bob Johnson had won the SCCA A-Production title in a Cobra.

Factory Cobras tackled Le Mans in 1963, although the combination of a new car and the team's unfamiliarity with Le Mans brought home predictably poor results. "We went from a club racing level, to a national and then International level in one season," said designer Pete Brock, Shelby's first employee and a key component in the Cobra's racing success.

Shelby loved racing, but he was also keenly aware of its promotional value. While his Cobras were all suitable for

COBRA SPORTS ROADSTER

271 HP Ford Fairlane 4V High Performance 289" Engine; Fully Synchronized Four Speed Manual Transmission; Hand Formed Aluminum Body; All Weather Road Equipment (Top, Tonneau Cover, Side Curtains); Full Instrumentation—Including Tachometer, Oil Temp., and Electric Clock; Windshield Washer and Electric Wipers; Directional Turn Indicators; Rack and Pinion Steering; Bucket Seats, covered in Genuine Leather; Powr-Lok Limited Slip Differential; 72 Spoke Wire Wheels with Knock-Off Hubs; Girling Disc Brakes, all Four Wheels; 7.35x15 Goodyear G-8 Tires;

Complete With Above Standard Equipment $5,995.00

FACTORY INSTALLED OPTIONAL EQUIPMENT AND ACCESSORIES

Tuned Air Cleaner—Chrome	$ 4.00
Aluminum Rocker Arm Covers	49.50
Front Grille Guard—Chrome	35.50
Rear Bumper Guard—Chrome	42.50
Exhaust Pipe Tips—Chrome	5.00
Adjustable Wind Wings	22.50
Tinted Sun Visors	19.50
Smith Heater	95.00
Competition Seat Belts, Ea.	16.50
White Side Wall Tires	42.00
Aluminum 4V Intake Manifold	71.00
Luggage Rack—Chrome	42.50
Outside Rear View Mirror	6.00
Custom AM Radio and Antenna	58.50
Chrome Wire Wheels	150.00
Detachable Hardtop	229.00
Deluxe Side Curtains	99.00

Competition Vehicles and Related High Performance Equipment (Prices Available on Request)
Prices and Specifications Subject to Change without Notice

SHELBY AMERICAN, INC. / 6501 W. IMPERIAL HWY. / LOS ANGELES, CALIF. 90045

DIMENSIONS

Wheelbase, In.	90.0
Tread Front, In.	51.5
Tread Rear, In.	52.5
Length Overall, In.	151.5
Width, In.	61.0
Height, In.	49.0
Frontal Area, Sq. Ft.	16.6
Ground Clearance, In.	5.0
Turning Circle, Ft.	34

SPECIFICATIONS

Curb Wt., Lbs.	2026
Distribution %	48/52
Tire Size	7.35x15
Brakes	Girling Disc
Engine Type and Size, Cu. In.	OHV-V8 289
Compression Ratio	11-1
BHP 5800 RPM	271

GEAR RATIOS

Differential	3.77
4th	1.00
3rd	1.41
2nd	1.78
1st	2.36

PERFORMANCE

Standing 1/4 Mile, Sec.	13.8
Standing 1/4 Mile, Speed	112
Top Speed, MPH	154

SCCA racing, most were purchased for street driving. Consequently, while throwing considerable effort into racing, Shelby also instituted several running changes that improved both the car's race and street manners. Some of the early running changes included the switch from worm-and-sector steering to rack-and-pinion steering, a change to a 3.77 rear differential gear, and, of course, the switch to the 289ci engine starting with the 76th car.

Shelby American grew explosively in 1963 and 1964. Shelby introduced the mid-engine King Cobra, a race-only special designed to take on increased competition in the USRRC. Street car sales were moving right along. Most importantly, Shelby mounted a serious effort in International GT competition: he wanted a World Championship, but he would have to take it at Ferrari's expense. The formidable Ferrari team dominated GT competition, winning the manufacturers' championship in nine of the previous eleven years.

While the Cobra was successful in most forms of sports car racing, it needed a more slippery body than the open coupe to be a threat to Ferrari. The solution was the Cobra Daytona Coupe, a Pete Brock-designed "Kammback" that conformed to FIA rules allowing custom body work over production car mechanicals. With the gorgeous and purposeful new sheet metal, the Daytona was good for the more than 180mph necessary for the Cobra to compete at high-speed tracks like Le Mans.

The Daytona Coupe made its debut at Daytona in early 1964 and scored its first GT class victory at Sebring in March. Daytona Coupes and other racing Cobras were quite successful that year although the Coupes came up short in the GT Championship battle when the Monza race was canceled, denying the Daytonas the chance to collect much needed points. The high speed Monza course and relatively short three-hour length of the race

OPPOSITE
Ford's brochure for the Cobra reads like a gearhead's dream. Hand-formed body, Girling disc brakes, 13.8sec quarter—all for about six grand.

NEXT PAGES
Only six Daytona Coupes were built. Shown is CSX2299, the second car constructed, which was finished at Carrozzeria Gran Sport in Italy. All of the hand-built coupes were slightly different from each other. This example was mistakenly assembled with a tall windshield and higher roof line—which turned out to be a blessing for tall driver Dan Gurney. CSX2299 was one of the two most successful Coupes, claiming such prizes as the GT class win at Le Mans in 1964 with Gurney and Bob Bondurant at the wheel.

"With guys like Holbert, Dave MacDonald, and Miles driving the thing we had such good feedback," designer Pete Brock remembers of the Daytona Coupe's development. And Ken Miles had more to contribute than just driving feedback. "Really all the design of the subframe was Ken's solution to stiffen the car. He'd had so many hours with the USRRC cars, knowing what they wouldn't do, he knew right away what to change in it. And under the rules, technically, that was all body stiffening. So, you know, if we'd built that body on a roadster it would have popped the windshield right out. They're that flexible," Brock said.

favored the Daytona Coupes and a win would have sealed the championship for Shelby. The cancellation smacked of politics, and Shelby made no bones about who was pulling the strings. "It was a face-saver to prevent the GT Ferraris from getting beaten by our Cobras, which they richly deserved and which they could not possibly have prevented," wrote Shelby.

Shelby came roaring back in 1965 with Daytonas and Cobras taking GT class victories at Daytona, Sebring, Monza, Oulton Park, the Nurburgring, the Rossfeld Hillclimb, Reims and the Coppa Di Enna. The success was especially sweet for Shelby, who finally beat his old rival Enzo Ferrari. With those victories, Shelby became the first American car maker to win the FIA World Manufacturers' Championship.

While the Daytona Coupes were bringing home the championship from overseas, the basic Cobra was about to take a major step in another direction. With the competition about to

The Daytona Coupe's 289ci engine produced around 385hp in racing trim with four downdraft Weber carburetors. The angled radiator allowed air to be funneled out through vents in the hood. Remarkably, after their retirement from racing, some of the Daytona Coupes were occasionally driven on the street.

Originally planned as a follow-up for the 289-powered Daytona Coupes, the Daytona Super Coupe was stillborn when Ford threw its weight behind the GT-40 project. This 427-powered Super Coupe, the only example ever made, sat unfinished until the early eighties when it was restored to blueprint specs with designer Pete Brock consulting. *Photo courtesy Super Ford magazine*

To qualify as a GT under FIA rules, the Daytona Coupe had to be able to carry a spare tire, just as a real road-going GT would. The Coupe's interior was often a less than hospitable place. Cockpit heat was a serious problem, especially in endurance races.

make drastic upgrades in performance (such as Chevrolet's 396ci Corvette) Shelby started making plans for the next generation of Cobras. Two things were certain—the next Cobra would need to be faster with improved suspension and chassis.

Despite the fact that some of the Shelby people wanted to use a larger displacement small-block engine, Ford was eager to showcase their 427ci big-block engine. Ford was heavily involved in the Shelby racing effort and the big-block fit in with the Cobra's performance image, so the project went ahead.

With Ken Miles handling development, a rough prototype was constructed and tested in early 1964. It was really not much more than a 427ci engine in a 289 chassis. Testing revealed that making a 427ci Cobra would require substantial changes to the chassis to accommodate an engine that large and powerful. A second prototype, built with an all-aluminum 390ci engine and raced in late 1964 at Nassau, proved more instructive.

To make it all work, Shelby American had to increase the diameter of the tubing on the chassis and make other reinforcements to strengthen the car's underpinnings. Coil springs replaced the 289 Cobra's outdated leaf springs. The new 427ci Cobra body was shorter, wider, and taller than the 289 models, and had a larger grille opening to improve engine cooling. Despite these changes, the car retained the distinctive Cobra lines.

Regular production of 427 Cobras began in January, 1965. Originally, the first 100 cobras were created for FIA GT racing, but not enough cars were built in time to qualify for the 1965 season and the rules were changed soon after to the 427's disadvantage anyway. Consequently, the unsold "competition" Cobras were badged as 427 S/C (Street/Competition or Semi-Competition) Cobras and marketed as brutally fast street cars, suitable for racing. The regular 427 street Cobras were put into production after the first batch of competition and S/C models.

Thanks to those sanctioned body-rule changes and the changing face of sports prototype racing, the 427 Cobras were never quite the success in big-time racing

The Ford GT-40 program sprang from the wreckage of Ford's attempt to purchase Ferrari in the early sixties. Unable to complete the merger, Ford decided to build its own exotic sports car for international racing and beat Ferrari at his own game. After struggling early, Ford handed the GT-40 racing program to Shelby in 1965. Shelby turned the program around, and GT-40s won at Le Mans in 1966 and 1967. Although successful, the GT-40 program was also a source of friction, as Shelby had to contend with both Ford's in-house racing people and with competing cars from Holman and Moody, another race shop with close ties to Ford. Pictured are Ken Miles and Bruce McLaren at Sebring in 1965. They finished in second place. *Dave Friedman Photo Collection*

Bill Neale—Capturing it on Canvas

Many people have tried to capture the essence of Shelby's cars in art, photography, and the printed word, but there's little argument about who is the acknowledged master of Shelby artwork—long time Shelby pal Bill Neale.

Like Shelby himself, Neale has been interested in racing and flying since he knew what cars and airplanes were. His aviation background includes a stint in the Navy in World War II, flying torpedo bombers in the Pacific.

As for cars, Neale still vividly remembers seeing his first auto race in the 1930s when an uncle took him to a race at Arlington Downs, a horse racing track. But California hot rods and his first glimpse of an MG truly fired Neale's appreciation for cars.

After graduating with a Bachelor of Arts degree from the University of North Texas, Neale received his formal art school training at the Chouinard Institute in Los Angeles. Neale's professional art career began in the advertising field, although he was painting cars while still in school. He worked at an agency as an illustrator and art director before starting Point Communications in 1970 where he still serves as Chairman of the Board. Virtually all of the well-known Neale paintings were done in his home office at night, after the day's work was done at the agency.

The first painting Neale did for a car magazine was a cover for *Road & Track* in the early sixties. Since then his illustrations have appeared in *Car and Driver*, *Automobile*, *Sports Cars Illustrated*, *Car Life*, and *Cycle World*. At one time, he kept a detailed record of his illustrations, but his journal was destroyed in a fire. By his own conservative estimate, he has created more than 1,000 serious car and motorcycle paintings, plus many minor illustrations.

Neale Speaks warmly of his relationship with shelby and his cars. "I think of any one person, I've probably done more of Shelby, and in a way it's just quite by accident really because we've just been friends so long," he says. "One of the first racing cars, sports racing cars, that I painted was of Shelby. Shelby was racing at Eagle Mountain Lake (in 1952), and I talked to him. He was driving a 2.0-liter Maserati and it was a really good race," Neale remembers. At that race there were several Chevy-powered specials that clearly out-classed Shelby's Maserati in power, but Shelby won on sheer driving skill. "And he asked me, he said, 'Would you paint me a picture?' and I said, 'Sure.' So that might very well have been one of the first commissions I ever did."

Bill Neale in his home studio, surrounded by decades of his artwork. He has tried, although display room is tight, to keep a few of his favorite originals for himself over the years. Cars are his favorite subject matter, but he enjoys painting motorcycles and aviation scenes as well.

Fast friends of Shelby, Bill and wife Nelda followed Shelby's career closely, even traveling to France in 1958 to see Shelby's Formula 1 race at Reims, which also turned out to be five-time world champion Juan Manuel Fangio's last race.

In 1959, Shelby, driving for the factory Aston Martin team, had his greatest triumph. Neale remembers his stateside vigil listening to the 24 Hours of Le Mans on the radio, "I was here in Dallas, and I was trying to get the news on the short wave radio, and I remember just listening to the race. When I found out that Shelby won, it was just a tremendously exciting thing."

Although Neale maintains Shelby is one of the best drivers he has seen, Shelby has always been a lot more than just a race car driver. "I've always thought of Shelby, first of all, as an entrepreneur, and a damn good one," Neale says. He also knows firsthand Shelby's proclivity for practical jokes, his golfing skills, and the fact that he still occasionally exercised his flying skills well into his seventies.

But despite all the legends, tall tales, and history associated with Carroll Shelby, Neale knows the central appeal of the cars—and why so many people want paintings and other mementos of Shelby's creations: "Take a 427 Cobra. There's not anything that will even come close to it even today. If you want to turn a bad day into something exciting, get in one of those darn old cars, be sure the wheels are pointed straight, and take off."

Bill Neale's painting "Cobra, 1965 World Manufacturers Champion." Neale usually works with acrylic paints or watercolors and offers the prints for sale in signed, limited editions. He has been closely tied with Shelby from the beginning, creating paintings of Shelby's driving career in the fifties, doing advertising work for Shelby American in the sixties, painting important moments in Shelby history, and working with Shelby's Heart Fund in the 1980s and 1990s. *Courtesy Bill Neale.*

The early 427 Cobras could be ordered from the factory in competition trim, which included the cut-down racing windshield, racing seat, racing brakes, and a competition-prepped aluminum 427ci engine with dry sump oiling. The roll bar, side pipes, racing mirrors, hood scoop, secondary oil cooler scoop, and twin aircraft batteries were already part of the S/C package.

that the 289 cars were. However there were certainly winners, such as Dick Smith's SCCA A-Production championships in 1966 and 1967. Also, with the extra weight of the big-block engine, the 427 cars didn't handle as well as the lighter 289 cars. Additionally, the 427 Cobra was much more expensive than the 289. The 427 Cobra's continuing fame grows from its unmatched performance on the street. Magazines clocked quarter mile times in the 12.4sec range, and the car's acceleration could only be described as brutal. The 427 Cobra has been rightly dubbed the fastest street car ever sold in America.

One of the generally unknown hidden facts about the 427 Cobra is that a lot of them were actually powered by slightly tamer 428s. The 425hp 427ci engines were expensive and in short supply, so Shelby equipped an undetermined number of Cobras with the dual-quad, 355hp 428ci engine. Although no match for a 427 on a race track exits, the 428 Cobras were still torquey, powerful engines that offered outstanding performance on the street.

In the end, increased safety regulations and emission controls killed the Cobra. Modern ideas of socially responsible transportation clashed with the pure performance nature of Shelby's creations. Plus, as a small manufacturer, complying with the endless rules that were coming down the pike would have taxed Shelby's resources to the breaking point, not to mention his patience.

When all is said and done, Shelby's Cobra legacy arose from a surprisingly small number of cars. The small-block, leaf spring Cobra's total production came to

Competition-prepared S/C Cobras received the side-oiler 427ci engine with medium-rise heads, radiator "puke tank," and Holman and Moody remote oil filter. Horsepower was in the neighborhood of 470 to 490. Competition and S/C Cobras both had an oil cooler mounted in the lower grille opening.

This 427 Cobra, CSX3022, was originally ordered and raced by Bob Grossman. It is one of the first fifty-two 427 Cobras built and was invoiced as an S/C with full factory competition prep. The car was raced heavily in SCCA A-Sedan competition in 1966 and also finished 10th overall at Sebring that year. Its racing career ended at Watkins Glen that year, when Grossman spun and hit a tree.

Racing and S/C Cobra interiors were stripped down even more than the already Spartan street Cobras. They had no glove box or door pockets, although no corners were cut on gauges.

655 cars, including street and race cars. When 427 Cobra production ended in the United States in late 1966, and in Britain in 1968, the coil spring, big-block car's production totaled 348. An automotive legend was built on the wheels of just a few cars.

Many competition Cobras are still raced in vintage racing events, like CSX3012, shown here at Sears Point in 1995 with Rick Titus at the wheel. Like all of the true competition 427 Cobras, CSX3012 has a colorful history. First purchased by Lother Motschenbacher, who raced the car but found it unreliable, so after a racing accident, he sold it back to Shelby American. The Cobra was refurbished at the Shelby plant, and then resold to another racer.

LEFT
The 427 S/C came with aluminum paneling in the trunk, plus twin Stewart Warner electric fuel pumps. S/C and full competition cars had 42gal gas tanks and pop-up gas caps, compared to 18gal tanks on street Cobras.

TWO

Mustangs Get Help

The introduction of the Mustang in 1964 was one of the all-time great success stories for Ford Motor Company. Demand for the car verged on a national hysteria, propelling sales past expectations by huge margins. The press was good and, in his autobiography *Iacocca*, long-time Ford and Chrysler honcho Lee Iacocca estimated Ford generated net profits of $1.1 billion on the Mustang in its first two years of production.

As with everything, however, there was room for improvement. One of the weak spots identified early by Ford strategists was the Mustang's lack of a high-performance image. Although certainly a sporty car, the Mustang didn't project muscle like many of the performance cars of the day. Most of the early Mustangs were sold with six-cylinder or eight-cylinder 289ci two-barrel engines. Despite the availability of 225 and 271hp four-barrel versions of the 289, the Mustangs had little or no performance image.

Ford was having great success with Shelby on the race track and wanted to draw on the Cobra magic to spice up

By the time 1970 rolled around, the GT350 Mustang certainly looked more aggressive than earlier models but was in fact a much more civilized machine. Since the 1970 models were simply leftover 1969 cars, the FBI was on hand to witness the destruction of the 1969 VIN tags and the installation of the 1970 tags.

The 1965 GT350 as sold new was just about a half-step away from being a full-blown race car.

OPPOSITE
A total of 561 Shelby GT350 were made in 1965, including prototypes, street cars, and race cars. All 1965 models are Wimbledon White with Guardsman Blue stripes; the over-the-hood "Le Mans" stripes were optional.

the Mustang. When Ford proposed the idea, Shelby accepted the challenge, convinced of the car's performance potential and the financial viability of the arrangement.

The deal was made. Ford sent semi-finished Mustangs to Shelby's facility in Venice, California, where Shelby would finish the cars in performance trim. The white Mustangs arrived without hoods, rear seats, exhaust systems, and minus regular Mustang and Ford identification. All cars were shipped to Shelby with the 271hp high-performance 289ci engine, T-10 four-speed transmission, a large nine-inch Detroit Locker rear end, and larger station wagon rear brakes.

Once in Shelby's hands, the Mustangs received suspension modifications perfected by Ken Miles. Among other changes these included relocated upper control arms, Koni shocks, a one-inch front sway bar, and traction bars. The 271hp 289 was bolstered with a liberal dose of Shelby performance parts, increasing the engine's horsepower rating to

The 1965 Shelby GT350 was powered by a 306hp version of Ford's 271hp high-performance 289ci engine. Shelby additions included Tri-Y headers, an aluminum high-rise intake manifold, and 715cfm carburetor, a 7.5qt finned aluminum oil pan, and Cobra valve covers. A "Monte Carlo bar" tied the inner fenders together, and a V-shaped "export brace" linked the shock towers to the firewall, all for the purpose of stiffening the chassis.

306. Unique Shelby parts such as a fiberglass hood and wooden Cobra steering wheel were installed. Also, Guardsman Blue GT-350 stripes created by Pete Brock were applied.

Two 1965 Shelby Mustang models were available: the GT350 and GT350R. Although the GT350R was the race version, neither model was particularly well suited for street use. All 1965 GT350s were sold with four-speed transmis-

The 1965 Shelby Mustang interior was all business, as you'd expect from a car built with racing in mind. Special Shelby features included competition seat belts and the unusual center-mounted dash pod that housed the oil pressure gauge and tachometer. The wood-rimmed steering wheel features a Shelby snake emblem.

Cragar 15x6 wheels made to Shelby specs were optional. The standard wheel was a regular production 15x5.5 station wagon wheel painted silver.

Shelby Mustangs received their own Shelby VIN plates, reflecting Shelby American's status as a small manufacturer rather than just an aftermarket tuner. The Shelby tag was affixed over Ford's VIN plate.

OPPOSITE
Shelby American had to build at least 100 GT350s to qualify the car for racing under SCCA B/Production rules, a task that was quickly accomplished. Since the rules allowed racing versions to have either suspension or engine modifications, but not both, Shelby concentrated his efforts on creating a race-ready suspension on the street car so he could modify the engines on the competition models. In B/Production, the GT350R competed against older Corvettes, Sunbeam Tigers and E-Type Jaguars. These competition Shelby Mustangs sold new for around $6,000. *Mike Mueller*

sions and no back seats (to better qualify for the SCCA's racing classes). Most had loud, side-exiting exhaust pipes as well. Some early cars were sold with trunk-mounted batteries, and luxuries like air conditioning were not available. A total of 561 1965 GT350s and GT350Rs were produced.

The GT350Rs were stripped of almost all amenities and made no pretense as street-going cars, with items such as the heater and defroster removed. Shelby American lightened the car by replacing the front bumper and steel valence with a fiberglass valence, removing the rear bumper, and replacing the glass in rear and door windows with Plexiglas. The competition models also received 34gal fuel tanks, electric fuel pumps, oversize radiators, and an oil cooler. The heads were ported and polished, and the engines were balanced and blueprinted. Only 36 GT350Rs were built in 1965. In that same year, a Shelby factory team car driven by Jerry Titus went on to win the SCCA's B-Production championship.

The 1965 model's rough, race-ready nature was great on the track, but at Ford's urging, the 1966 GT350s were toned down a bit. Both air conditioning and Ford's high-perfor-

Only 36 1965 GT350R Mustangs were built. This car, No. 5R534, was built in the final of three batches and remains one of the most original in existence. Like many of the competition cars, it was raced in amateur events until being retired, and then run in occasional vintage races. Shelby lightened the GT350R wherever possible, using a fiberglass hood, fiberglass front valence, no rear bumper, Plexiglas rear and side windows, and light aluminum panels to replace the rear quarter vents. *Mike Mueller*

mance C-4 automatic transmission were optional. Five colors were available that year with Candy Apple Red, Raven Black, Sapphire Blue, and Ivy Green joining Wimbledon White on the option list. The GT350 was fitted with a back seat and some of the more serious high-performance features, such as the Detroit Locker rear differential, were made optional. But not everything was a step away from performance—a Paxton supercharger joined the option list in 1966.

Production increased dramatically in 1966. Compared to 561 the previous year, 2,378 1966 GT350s were produced. A large part of that increase was due to an unusually large sale to one customer— Hertz Rent-A-Car. Shelby employee

The GT350R's high-performance 289 was bolstered with cylinder heads modified by Valley Head Service, a hotter cam, straight exhaust, racing oil pan, an oil cooler, and an oversize radiator. Horsepower was around 350. *Mike Mueller*

On the GT350R interior the factory Ford instrumentation was replaced by Shelby-spec instrumentation. The glove box door and carpet were deleted as part of the weight-saving program. Most cars came with a lightweight racing bucket seat as well. *Mike Mueller*

Most of the Hertz GT350H cars were black with gold stripes, although some were made in other colors. Prominent Hertz identification included wheel center caps that read "Hertz Sports Car Club." Also prominent was a dash-mounted sticker warning customers that the car was equipped with competition brakes, and would require higher than normal pedal pressure. All 1966 Shelbys received the Plexiglas rear quarter window in place of the standard vented panel.

OPPOSITE
By the late sixties, Carroll Shelby was marketing a full line of accessories. This 1967 advertisement shows that, besides performance parts, everything from matchbooks to beer glasses was available from Shelby Accessories. Many of the items commemorated Team Shelby's 1965 FIA GT World Championship.

Peyton Cramer had approached Hertz about adding the Shelby Mustang to the Hertz line-up, and eventually received orders for 1,000 Shelbys, which were designated GT350H. Two prototypes were built, and all of the 1,000 ordered were eventually shipped.

For 1967, the Mustang received its first major redesign, resulting in a slightly larger, and heavier car. One of the reasons the Mustang was enlarged was to accomodate Ford's big-block engine. The competing manufacturers were packing big-blocks into their muscle cars, and Ford wasn't about to fall behind. GM introduced the Camaro and Firebird in 1967, with available 396 and 400ci engines. Also, Plymouth's Barracuda was sporting increasingly large engines.

The Shelby Mustang reflected the changes made in the Mustang line, especially under the hood. The regular Mustang GT could accommodate Ford's 390ci engine, so Shelby American stuffed the dimensionally identical 428 under the hood and created the GT500. The GT500's 428ci powerplant was Ford's Police Interceptor engine fitted with an aluminum 427 "medium riser" intake manifold and two

Stuffing a big-block 428ci engine into the Mustang proved to be a good move for Shelby, as the new GT500 outsold the small-block GT350 2,048 units to 1,175. By 1967, ten exterior colors were available, including the Brittany Blue seen on this model. Also new were the striking grille-mounted headlights.

The 1967 GT500's dual-quad, 428ci Police Interceptor engine was rated at 355hp. That was enough to propel the car through the quarter mile in 14.5sec at 101 mph, according to the May, 1967, issue of *Motor Trend.* A GT500 with automatic transmission was good for a 14.9sec ET in the same test. This engine is in award-winning condition.

600cfm four-barrel carburetors. The GT350 retained its 306 horsepower 289 although the engines lost their Tri-Y headers in favor of regular Hi-Po 289 exhaust manifolds.

The Shelby Mustangs had more than large engines to set them apart from lesser Mustangs that year. More effort was made to give the Shelby cars their own distinct look, too. The rear deck is a unique Shelby item, which was combined with 1967 Cougar taillights to give a clean, and attractive look. The 1967 Shelby also had a unique hood and nose, in addition to Shelby-only wheels. Also of note is that 1967 was the first year of production for the Shelby de Mexico Mustangs. Shelby and businessman Eduardo Velazquez formed a partnership that year that resulted in the creation of more than 600 street cars for the Mexican market produced from 1967 to 1969.

Besides having the first big-block engine in a Shelby Mustang, the 1967s are remembered as the last Shelby Mustangs built at Shelby's California facility. As production increased, Shelby American's ability to keep up was strained, causing Ford to push for a transfer of production to Michigan where it could offer more mass production assistance. Additionally, finding a high quality source for the

With ever-increasing competition in the performance car market in 1967, Ford was all too happy to associate their regular production Mustangs with Shelby's creations. With the Mustang's first redesign that year, the Mustang GT was available with Ford's 390ci big-block engine, while Shelby Mustangs offered "Le Mans developed" 428ci big-blocks.

larger quantities of fiberglass pieces used by Shelby was an issue. The better sources were up north.

Consequently, when the 1968 Shelby Mustangs rolled off the assembly line, they were rolling off the assembly line of the A.O. Smith Company in Ionia, Michigan. As part of the move, Shelby American split into three groups in two locations: parts and racing operations were handled in Torrance, California, and Mustang production headquarters were in Livonia, Michigan.

As the company was changing, the 1968 models also evolved. The 1968 Shelby Mustangs were the first offered in convertible form (although four convertibles were reportedly built as specials in 1966). The dual-quad, Police Interceptor 428 was replaced by the new single four-barrel 428

Very few 1967 Shelbys were built with a white interior; most came with a black or tan (Parchment) interior scheme. The 1967 Shelbys had a wood-rimmed steering wheel unique to that year, and a gauge pack mounted under the center of the dash.

The coiled snake emblem was new for 1967. Carroll Shelby sold the rights to the "Cobra" name to Ford in the sixties, and consequently the coiled snake and Cobra name have been recognizable symbols used on Mustangs manufactured long after Shelby and Ford parted company. Mustang II, Cobras IIs, and King Cobras used the handle in the seventies, and Special Vehicle Team (SVT) Mustang Cobras used the name from 1993–96.

In 1967 Shelby produced 26 notchback Group 2-spec Mustangs for Trans-Am and A-Sedan racing. The first five were the prototype and factory team cars and the rest were sold to racing-minded customers. Pictured is the seventh car built, raced early in its career by privateers Mary Ellen Wilkins and Merle Brennan. The car saw mostly A-Sedan action, but was reportedly raced in West Coast Trans-Am events in the late sixties and early seventies. The car was sold to a Mexican owner in 1974, who raced it in Mexico in a variety of sedan classes. When the car was purchased by its current owner in 1988, it was just a shell and required total restoration. Many of the cars had similar histories, racing in a variety of classes and then disappearing for long periods of time.

The 1967 Trans-Am Mustangs prepared by Shelby used a quick-open gas cap mounted near the center of the trunk lid, along with a splash shield and an oversize gas tank. Many of the parts from the GT350R adapted easily to the 1967 racers.

Cobra Jet engine. The GT500 renamed the GT500KR, "KR" standing for King of the Road. The 289 in the GT350 was replaced by a larger, but less powerful, 250hp 302 which gave the 1968 GT350 the dubious distinction of being the least powerful Shelby car made—at least until Shelby started working with four-cylinder Dodges in the 1980s. The year 1968 did represent a high point in Shelby Mustang sales with 4,450 units built and sold.

From there, sales came harder. Besides increased competition from GM and Chrysler, Shelby's Mustangs were facing increasing competition from other Mustang performance models, as well as Mercury's Cougar. When the 1969 Shelbys were introduced, they were no longer the only hot Mustang on the lot. In 1969, Ford saturated the market with their own Boss 302 Mustang, a 375hp Boss 429, and the Mach one, available with the potent 428 Cobra Jet. Even the Mustang GT was still in the line up, available with a variety of performance engines.

Still the Shelby Mustangs soldiered on. The 1969 models were again the GT350 and GT500, available in convertible or fastback (Sportsroof) configuration. The GT350 had Ford's new 351 Windsor four-barrel under the hood, while the GT500 retained its 335hp 428 Cobra Jet engine. If anything, the 1969 Shelbys looked even more aggressive than their predecessors, thanks to more unique body parts than ever before. The cars had their own unique fiberglass fenders, loop front bumpers, five-scoop hoods, and fiberglass deck lids and rear panels. The reflective side stripes added to the bold look, as did the various coiled Cobra emblems that popped up all over the Shelby's interior and exterior.

Near the end of 1969, Shelby officially asked Ford to end the partnership between the two companies. Starting as early

The 1967 Shelby Group 2 cars featured race-prepped 289ci engines, complete with GT-40 heads, twin 600cfm carbs, R-Model valve covers, racing cam and headers, and a Cobra scatter shield. This car features a handmade air box identical to the type the factory Shelby team cars used.

Ford won the 1967 SCCA Trans-Am manufacturers' championship thanks largely to the efforts of Shelby team driver Jerry Titus. Titus is shown dicing with Parnelli Jones at Daytona in February 1967. Titus finished fourth. He went on to win four races that season, enough to narrowly best Mark Donohue in the Roger Penske Camaro for the season championship. *Dave Friedman Photo Collection*

OPPOSITE
Although dozens of factory 427-powered Shelby GT500 Mustangs are rumored to have been built, in reality probably less than ten were—and verifiable documentation of even those is in short supply. One definitely legitimate 427 GT500 is the "Super Snake," created by Mel Burns Ford in Long Beach, California, and Shelby American. Built as a prototype for a proposed run of fifty 427 Shelby Mustangs, the car's high price kept the project from moving forward. The Super Snake shown here was the only one built by the dealer. It was later used for high-speed tire testing by Goodyear, reaching speeds up to 170 mph. *Mike Mueller*

as 1967, Shelby began to lose interest in the Mustang enterprise. As the Mustang got larger and heavier, its racing career was essentially over and so was much of Shelby's enthusiasm. Also, over the years Ford gradually became more involved with the daily operations of Shelby's business, and if ever there was a man who disliked dealing with a corporate bureaucracy, it was Carroll Shelby. Dealing with the endless layers of vice presidents and cost accountants, or "bean counters" as Shelby calls them, left him burned out and irritated. No doubt this feeling was partly mutual. The futher prospect of dealing with upcoming government emissions and safety regulations didn't exactly fill Shelby with enthusiasm. Ford management agreed to the break up.

Then where did the 1970 Shelby Mustangs come from? All 1970 Shelbys are essentially renumbered and rebadged 1969 models. With sales on the slow side, several 1969 models were still backed up in the production pipeline at the end of the model year. Rather than send them to dealers as brand new year-old cars, Ford and Shelby decided to give them new 1970 VIN tags and offer them as 1970 models. The cars were given new front spoilers and twin black hood stripes to help differentiate them from the previous year's offerings.

The Super Snake's side-oiler 427 featured aluminum heads, intake manifold, and water pump and spun the dyno to a staggering 520hp. Besides the Super Snake, the number of special order Mustangs produced by Shelby with 427s between their fenders can probably be counted on the fingers of two hands, maybe less. Several dealers offered 427 engine swaps though. Thus 1967 GT500s with 427s under the hood show up from time to time. *Mike Mueller*

OPPOSITE
In 1967, Shelby shifted their emphasis a bit by taking advantage of the slightly wider engine bay in the new Mustang body to offer the big block-powered GT500, which was more of a classic grand touring sports car (American style) than the race-oriented GT350. The GT500 was equipped with a dual quad version of the 428ci police interceptor engine.

Do you agree with Carroll Shelby that good driving is a fine art? Then these all new 1967 Shelby GT cars are custom crafted for you. By incorporating his competition-proved design and engineering features in the Mustang, Carroll Shelby has created two unique road performers that carry the *lowest* price tags of *any* true GT cars.

The GT 500 features a brand-new Cobra LeMans dual 4-barrel engine, developed from the V-8 that powered the 1966 LeMans winners. GT 350 power comes from the high performance Cobra 289 with free-breathing Shelby induction and exhaust. All-synchro four-speed box or heavy-duty Cruise-O-Matic are optional on both cars.

These goodies make your Shelby GT one of the *safest* cars you can drive: Massive disc front and air-cooled drum rear brakes. Shelby-modified suspension for 30% less cornering roll. Crisp 16-to-1 power steering*. LeMans-proved wide tread nylon super-safety tires. Integral roll bar*, double shoulder harness*, quick-release seat belts and eye level brake and turn indicator lights.

Naturally, you'll find true GT features. Unique Shelby styling. Luxury interior with bucket seats, complete instrumentation, wood rim steering wheel, folding rear seat*.

You should expect a lot from a car built by America's first F.I.A. World's Champion. You'll get all you expect when you drive a Shelby GT 350 or GT 500. One is waiting at your Shelby dealer's now.

SHELBY G.T. 350 and 500 The Road Cars

Powered by Ford

Shelby American, Inc., 6501 West Imperial Highway, Los Angeles, Calif. 90009. Builders of the Cobra, Manufacturers of Cobra high performance parts and kits. *optional at extra cost

The GT500KR convertible is among the most recognized and sought-after Shelby Mustangs, a noteworthy achievement considering only 318 were built. It would appear the "King of the Road" label has stayed in people's minds, as has the aggressive look generated by the fiberglass hood with forward mounted scoops, driving lights, and handsome plastic-covered roll bar. Fastback KRs were more plentiful with 933 built. Earlier in 1968, 1,140 GT500 fastbacks were built.

Very few 1968 GT500KRs came with the four-speed transmission because the Shelby Mustang was by then moving steadily toward luxury gran touring status. This one is a rarity. This car also has the optional tilt-away steering wheel. The 1968 Shelbys had a slick coiled snake embossed in the vinyl armrest.

Thus ended the Shelby Mustang saga, with leftover cars languishing on dealer lots. In fact, it is likely that if Shelby's Mustangs hadn't faded away in 1970, they undoubtedly would have within a couple years anyway as the entire performance car market was dead by 1973 thanks to rising insurance rates and higher gas prices. As for Shelby, he was relieved to be away from the auto business. He went on vacation, and started planning his next business ventures.

To help separate the Shelbys from their more pedestrian Mustang brethren, the 1968 Shelby got unique appearance features such as sequential taillights from the 1965 Thunderbird and unique fiberglass body panels. Quad exhaust tips were standard on GT500KRs. Attractive ten-spoke wheels were optional.

For 1968, the GT500 started the year with a single four-barrel version of the Police Interceptor 428. Later, the 428 Cobra Jet Ram Air engine was installed when the new GT500KR was introduced (shown here). The Cobra Jet had 427 low-riser heads and other internal differences that set it apart from the Police Interceptor version—plus primitive smog equipment. Although horsepower was down, on paper, from 360 to 335, performance was not. *Hot Rod* magazine fiddled with tire pressures and belts and coaxed an automatic transmission KR convertible through the quarter mile in 14.58 seconds, a lighter four-speed fastback model in 14.01 seconds.

RIGHT
In a departure from earlier all-business Shelby Mustangs, 1969 models were slathered in wood grain trim, which was supposed to impart an air of sophistication to the big gran touring coupes. An altered Mercury Cougar console with inset gauges helped set the Shelby's interior apart from other Mustangs.

OPPOSITE
The 1969 GT500 carried over the under-rated 335 horsepower 428 Cobra Jet engine from the 1968 models. The cars could be optioned with the "Drag Pak," which changed the engine designation to Super Cobra Jet, and offered an oil cooler and lower rear differential gears, up to a 4.30 with Detroit Locker.

A total of 789 Shelby Mustangs were converted over from 1969 spec to 1970 models. The 1970 models can be distinguished by their twin, black hood stripes and front chin spoiler.

For 1969 and 1970, the GT350's engine was the four-barrel 351ci Windsor, rated at 290hp and 385lb-ft of torque. Setting it apart from lesser 351s in other Mustangs was Ram Air induction and an aluminum intake manifold, plus Cobra dress-up features.

The 1970's interior was festooned with all manner of Cobra emblems, such as this one the door panel. There were virtually no differences between 1969 and 1970 interiors.

OPPOSITE
This ad for the 1965 GT350 captures the race-ready image of the early Shelby Mustangs.

The Hurst Shifter in this interior is an aftermarket piece, but otherwise the interior is pure 1970 Shelby. Finding a manual transmission shifter of any kind was a rarity in the 1970 GT350 because most were equipped with automatic transmissions.

A unique feature of the 1969 and 1970 Shelbys was the distinctive center outlet exhaust. The 1970 models continued to use the 1965 Thunderbird taillights introduced in 1968. The 1969 and 1970 convertibles kept their roll bars, but they were not as thick as on the 1968 convertibles and were not as integrated into the chassis.

THREE

Dodge Days

After his travails in the late 1960s with Ford Motor Company's bureaucracy, Shelby stayed out of the auto manufacturing business during the 1970s and early 1980s. Chili and cornbread mixes, wheels, and other business ventures bore his name, and by the late 1970s, it was beginning to look as if the great Shelby Mustangs and Cobras of the 1960s would be his final automotive legacy.

Concurrently, the Chrysler Corporation was very nearly getting out of the auto manufacturing business, although not voluntarily. Shoddy quality, poor designs, and bad business practices had placed America's number three automaker a couple steps away from joining Studebaker and Packard on the junk heap of once-great marques.

When Lee Iacocca signed on as Chrysler CEO on November 2, 1978, he faced the daunting tasks of reversing the company's financial slide, improving its products, instituting modern business practices, and resurrecting Chrysler's plummeting reputation. His solutions—in addition to government

Market conditions in the 1980s were radically different from the 1960s, and Shelby's Dodges reflected those changes. Front-wheel drives and turbochargers were in, while V-8-powered sports cars were out. The Shelby Lancer and Shelby Dakota pickup truck were typical of Shelby's work with Chrysler.

This early Shelby Charger design concept, dated 1982, accurately indicates the direction the 1983 car would eventually take, although the side-exiting exhaust never made it to production. The C-pillar panel, Shelby wheels, and front air dam were unique Shelby pieces upon introduction. *Chrysler Corporation*

loan guarantees—included economical, if plain, K-cars, minivans, and various rebadged Mitsubishi products. Ever the salesman, Iacocca also knew the company needed to offer more than just bread-and-butter transportation. Chrysler needed some flash, a performance image, something to attract younger buyers, and Iacocca knew a good place to get it—Carroll Shelby.

Since Lee Iacocca had been one of the handful of Ford executives that Shelby had trusted, his jump to Chrysler was not much of a leap. After all, what Iacocca was proposing was essentially the same sort of gig Shelby had at Ford: converting production sedans converting into genuine performance cars that wouldn't require World Bank funding to purchase. Shelby signed on with Chrysler in 1982.

The new partnership began modestly. Product development was carried out at a new Chrysler Shelby Performance Center, later renamed the Dodge Shelby Performance Center, in Santa Fe Springs, California. As a Chrysler facility instead of an actual Shelby skunk works, all manner of experimental

front-wheel drive vehicles were tested and scrutinized at the Performance Center. Shelby's influence soon became apparent: in fact, the first Shelby Dodge hustled through the development process in a quick three months.

The first vehicle to receive Shelby's name was the 1983 Dodge Shelby Charger, a three-door hatchback spun off the L-Body Omni chassis. The front-wheel drive Charger and its 2.2-liter overhead-cam four-cylinder engine had been introduced a few years before. It had served as a sporty, if pedestrian, out-

The Dodge-built Shelby Chargers were far more numerous than their black and silver Shelby-built counterparts. From 1983–87 the Dodge Shelby Chargers were available in silver over blue, blue over silver, silver over black, and silver over red, like this 1987. The Dodge Shelby Chargers had the Turbo I engine in 1986, rated at 146 horsepower.

Originally planned for 1985, the Omni GLHS was introduced in June 1986, as a 1986-and-a-half model. The Omni GLHS had the best power-to-weight ratio of the Shelby Dodges, and thus Shelby Automobiles started off at the high point.

post in the barren Chrysler landscape. At the time, with the heavier K-chassis Dodge Daytona still months from production, it was the sportiest car in Chrysler's line-up, and the most likely platform to receive the performance car treatment. Released mid-year to generally positive reviews, the Shelby Charger was developed at the Performance Center, but built on the same production line as regular econo-Chargers.

Although the ads for the Shelby Charger cried, "It ain't just paint," largely it was at least at first. Available in two striking paint schemes, Santa Fe Blue on Radiant Silver or the reverse, the 1983 Shelby Charger's 16.8 seconds quarter mile didn't quite back up its muscle car looks, at least compared to Shelby's past. Yet, the car was not without potential. The Chrysler Shelby Performance Center quickly developed some of that potential by improving the 2.2's horsepower from 94 to 107, raising the compression ratio from 9.6:1 to 9.1, altering the cam timing and spark advance, and enriching the mixture on the Holley two-barrel carburetor. The final drive ratio was a low 3.87:1 compared to the stock 3.56:1. The suspension received shorter and stiffer springs, and 195/50VR-15 Goodyear Eagle GT tires. Curb weight came in at 2388lbs.

If the 1983 models weren't exactly the high point of Carroll Shelby's career, at least the Charger continued to evolve. In 1985, Chrysler's 146hp Turbo I engine became the standard powerplant in the Shelby Charger, and *Motor Trend* saw quarter mile times drop to 16.10sec at 85.8 mph. The car also received larger rear brakes, Monroe Formula GP gas shocks and struts, equal length half-shafts, and strengthened internals in the transmission. Having increased the horsepower, the Charger started being compared with V-8-powered Mustangs and Camaros instead of with Volkswagen GTIs.

As the Shelby Charger grew into a real performance car, the Shelby operation grew with it. In the mid-1980s Shelby

One thing the GLHS had in common with early Shelby Mustangs was a no-nonsense, all-business interior. The Omni was Dodge's entry-level economy car, and it showed in the simple interior trim. Note the Shelby dash plaque, which bore Carroll Shelby's signature and the sequential number of the car.

The Omni GLHS debuted the 2.2-liter Turbo II engine in the Shelby line. The Turbo II boasted 175hp, thanks to an air-to-air intercooler, Shelby-designed manifold, and 12psi of boost. This engine has two non-stock pieces, the polished valve cover and red plug wires.

realized that the market was right for selling genuine limited production specialty cars, much as Shelby American had done in the 1960s. Thus, Shelby Automobiles in Whittier, California, was born. It was a separate facility with its own employees. Suddenly, Shelby Dodges weren't just tape-striped and fat-tired Chryslers, but real genuine Shelby automobiles from a genuine Shelby facility.

Tim Pettijohn moved to California in 1988 to work with Shelby Automobiles, and served as National Performance Parts manager until the end of the company in 1990. As Performance Parts manager, he had responsibility for overseeing the Shelby Performance parts catalog and providing technical support to Shelby's dealer network and customers. From Pettijohn's point of view, Shelby Automobiles had a lot in common with Shelby American, right down to the employees. "A couple people that were at Shelby Automobiles worked with him when he was doing the Fords back in the sixties," Pettijohn recalled.

The circumstances may have been similar, but there were no V-8s or rear-wheel drive cars this time around.

The first car created at the new Shelby plant was the 1986 Omni GLHS, introduced in June of 1986. The GLHS was the final evolution of the Omni GLH (Goes Like Hell) series, a Shelby-inspired econo-rod introduced in 1984. With a light suspension, P195/50HR-15 tires, and the Shelby Charger's high-output 2.2, rated at 110hp, the 1984 GLH was one of the quickest small cars of its time. It became even quicker with the introduction of the Turbo I engine in 1985.

The GLHS Chargers were delivered to Shelby from Chrysler with the silver stripe down the side, as the production run was made specifically for Shelby. The advertised base price for the GLHS Charger was $12,995. According to the Shelby brochure, the Charger GLHS was good for 14.7sec quarter miles and could hold .84g on the skid pad.

Shelby's first stab at a sophisticated four-door sedan, the Shelby Lancer listed for $16,995 and had a claimed top speed of 135mph with quarter mile times quoted at 15.7sec. The car was taken to task by the press when new for being a bit on the crude side due to its harsh ride and high noise levels.

The Lancer was powered by the 2.2-liter Turbo II engine, rated at 175hp and 175lb-ft of torque.

OPPOSITE
The 1988 CSX-T rented for $34.95 per day from Thrifty. A regular production 1988 CSX was planned, but never put into production. According to Tim Pettijohn, all 1988s went to Thrifty, except one that was sold to a dealership in Connecticut. This particular CSX-T wears a prototype set of composite wheels. This is one of only two sets produced, as the Fiberide wheels were a different design.

To convert a GLH to a GLHS, Shelby added an air-to-air intercooler, a Shelby-designed intake manifold and cranked the turbo boost up to 12psi. The result was 175hp. Larger 205-series tires were added along with gas-charged Koni Shocks and struts. "It was the intention for our car to come out in 1985, but there were a lot of

top executives at Chrysler that were concerned about 175hp in a front-wheel drive car," Pettijohn said. "I think Carroll finally got the right guy to drive it and he kind of gave it a go."

The first car out of Shelby's facility, the Omni GLHS, also turned out to be the lightest and quickest of the Shelby Dodges. *Car and Driver* clocked one at 14.9sec at 93 mph through the quarter mile in their April 1986 issue—making

The Thrifty Rental Shelby CSX-Ts were powered by the 150hp 2.2-liter Turbo I engine. This car is fitted with aftermarket plug wires and a K&N air filter, plus a retrofit intercooler.

The angular Shadow interior housed its share of Shelby emblems, including a dash plaque, steering wheel logo, and door sill emblems. Note the special Thrifty sunglasses that came with the CSX-T

The stylized "race track" Shelby logo was a constant throughout the Shelby Dodge era, appearing on seat upholstery, emblems, even on accessories and brochures.

The Shelby Dakota's 175hp 318ci engine (5.2 liter) represented the only V-8 of the modern Shelby era. The Shelby Dakota used electric cooling fans since the Dakota's front end wasn't extended for regular production V-8 use until 1991, and room was tight. The electric fans freed up five more horsepower. Otherwise, the throttle body injected engine was the same as the stock Ram truck engine. Shelby Automobiles later offered a performance kit for the V-8 that boosted power about 25hp.

the GLHS quicker than the last couple years of GT350 production. The GLHS is also one of the rarer Shelbys, with only 500 units built—fewer even, than the number of 1965 GT350 Mustangs.

"The next car that was scheduled to come out was supposed to be the 1987 Shelby Lancer," Pettijohn said. "The car originally was going to be in that charcoal gray metallic color because we felt that in order to go after the BMW five-series it should be a more relaxed color." Production of the Lancer, however, was delayed for corporate reasons. Pettijohn explained, Chrysler, in their continuing political crop dust, decided that they didn't have time to do our run of Lancers when they wanted to, and kept delaying us, delaying us, and delaying us in the end we decided to build the 1987 Charger GLHS since we already had everything done for the Omni. This was actually probably the only car that Shelby Automobiles produced that actually came out with all the other new cars."

As a result of delays in the Lancer production, the Charger GLHS was introduced in September, 1986, as an 1987 model, giving it the benefit of being part of Chrysler's regular new-car introduction. Pettijohn recalls that "The Charger was kind of a

car that was thrown in-between to make up for the lack of Chrysler supplying us with the Lancers on time." Because the Charger and Omni were mechanically identical under the skin, it took no special engineering feat to create the GLHS, and thus a quick turnaround was possible. Shelby Automobiles produced 1000 GLHS Chargers.

The next car out of the chute was the oft-delayed Shelby Lancer. The Shelby Lancer was introduced in February 1987. This car was intended to do battle with higher-priced and more sophisticated European imports. It is also the only four-door (five-door if you count the hatch) sedan of Shelby's career. Although it is generally reported that 800 Shelby

The Shelby Dakota color options were but two—red with black trim or white with black trim. White trucks are the rarer of the two, with only 495 built, compared to 995 red trucks.

Lancers were produced, the actual number created was 780 (380 with automatic transmissions) and 400 with manual transmissions. According to Pettijohn, all the automatic cars (with the exception of a few oddballs) also came with a leather interior, and they were $1000 more MSRP than the manual cars with the cloth interior.

That year was a busy one for Shelby Automobiles because a third car was produced later in 1987: the CSX, based on the Dodge Shadow. Like the Lancer, the Shadow was based on K-car architecture as opposed to the Omni and Charger's L-body origins. The 1987 CSX had the Turbo II engine under the hood, with its intercooled turbocharged powerplant good for 175hp. Only 750 were produced, all with the base Shadow interior with half-console and manual transmission. The CSX was introduced in late March of 1987.

After the burst of productivity spread over three car lines in 1987, all of 1988's production was focused on one car line for one customer—Thrifty Rental Car. Much like the GT350H Mustangs built for Hertz Rental, the 1988 CSX-T was built specifically to give the Rental Car company an image boost. Although 1000 cars were reportedly built, a search of the VINs by Pettijohn revealed only 999 produced for Thrifty.

All Thrifty CSX-T are Turbo I cars, and thus are not intercooled. Thrifty selected this package largely because Chrysler's factory warranty was substantially better than Shelby's. According to Pettijohn, "We merely added the ground effects package, added the rim and tire combination to the vehicle and added the Monroe Formula GPs" There were plans for another run of Thrifty CSXs for 1989, but the deal never came together.

In 1989, Shelby Automobiles branched out again, this time anointing the mid-size Dakota pickup with the Shelby treatment and producing the most advanced run of CSXs yet. Although the high-tech CSX stole the headlines at the

The last Shelby-badged Dodge was this 1991 2.5-liter turbo Daytona. Ordered after Shelby production had ended, the car was supposed to be switched to the new IROC trim, but was shipped to the owner with both Shelby identification and an IROC I.D. tag. The car's window sticker identified the car as a Dodge Daytona Shelby IROC, so the last Shelby Dodge built was also the second IROC Daytona built. Instead of finishing with a bang, the Shelby Dodge saga ended with the St. Louis plant manager calling the car owner to apologize for the mix-up. *Courtesy Mopar Muscle magazine.*

Carroll Shelby's role in the development of the Viper led Dodge to chose him to drive the pace car at the 1991 Indianapolis 500. It was only fitting that the man responsible for the original Cobra should have a hand in creating its 1990s counterpart. *Chrysler Corporation*

time, the Shelby Dakota turned out to have the longest lasting impact. Shelby Automobiles' work with the Dakota foreshadowed Chrysler's future product plans, as their engineering paved the way for fitting Chrysler's popular line of "Magnum" V-8 engines in the Dakota starting in 1991.

Shelby Automobiles built the first prototype V-8 Dakotain during the truck's debut year in 1987. The Shelby Dakota turned out to be much more than just bolt-on engine and suspension parts and tape stripes. "That was probably the most intensive project that we undertook," Pettijohn remembered. "We actually had to start welding to the

The Dodge-Shelby cars are spec racers, with the cars powered by identical, sealed, 255hp, 3.3 liter Dodge V-6 engines. Only gear ratio changes, suspension set-up, and wing adjustments are allowed.

Carroll Shelby stepped back into the racing arena in 1992 with an SCCA spec racer series that carried his name. Originally named the Shelby Can-Am and later changed to the SCCA Dodge/Shelby Pro Series, the race cars represented his belief that money shouldn't rule racing. The cars are all single seat, open cockpit cars held to identical specifications. Shown is Augie Pabst III.

The inaugural six-race 1992 Dodge Shelby Pro Series season was won by Scott Harrington. Kyle Konzer, who had lost the championship in 1992 by a single point, took the 1993 title. Shown is Chris Winkler driving to victory at the 1994 Dallas Grand Prix. It was the second win of his career.

K-frame. The trucks were ordered from Chrysler with the V-6, and the V-6s were removed from the vehicle and shipped back to Chrysler for warranty engines."

The V-8 consisted of Chrysler's throttle-body injected 318, hooked to an automatic transmission. The Shelby Dakota with V-8 was quick and powerful, but later Dodge trucks would pack more horsepower and better performance. Shelby had high hopes for the Dakota, however, and development of an outrageous twin turbo V-8 was undertaken. Jack Roush handled much of the twin turbo V-8's development, which was penciled in as a possible 1990 or 1991 model. It would be dubbed the Shelby AK-1, a polite acronym for "Ass Kicker."

While the Dakota allowed the Shelby crew to play with V-8s and rear-wheel drive once again, the CSX broke ground with two engineering firsts. The 1989 CSX was the first production car built that rolled on composite wheels, made from compression-molded fiberglass. It was also the first American production car manufactured with a variable-nozzle turbocharger(VNT), which provided in one unit the benefits of both a large turbo, with high flow rates, and a small turbo, with quicker response lower in the rev range. The horsepower rating for the VNT engine, designated Turbo IV, was the same as the Turbo II, 175, but the VNT engine offered better torque and responsiveness.

As it turned out, these breakthroughs eventually ended up as footnotes rather than stepping stones, because the 1989 CSX was the last car Shelby Automobiles produced. "In all reality, out of the 500 that claimed to be produced on the 1989 CSXs, there were only really 498 produced," Pettijohn remembers, "because two of the production cars were pulled off the line and were converted paint-wise to become 1990 model press cars—which were going to be the sixteen-valve CSX. Of course, that car never happened."

If Shelby had continued production into the nineties, his Dodges would have been the best yet. Shelby Automobiles had been working for years on a Turbo III engine, a double overhead cam, sixteen-valve powerplant that would have produced more than 220 horsepower in production trim. The engines were to have been supplied by Chrysler Mexico, with help from old Shelby pal Eduardo Velazquez.

Several factors conspired to kill that car. "The thing that killed Shelby Automobiles was the 1990 car," estimates Pettijohn. "It was too expensive to build the 1990 car the way we wanted to build it—have Chrysler Mexico do this and do that and add a leather Recaro interior was expensive. We sent the car to Chrysler in October of

1989 for final budget approval. They looked at the Shadow said, 'Well you know, in order for you guys to sell this and make any kind of money, you're going to have to MSRP this car for $22,000. And we could be wrong, but we don't think too many people are going to pay $22,000 for a Shadow.' So Chrysler advised strongly against it, and said that if they had problems selling those particular cars they weren't going to bail us out this time. At that point in time Carrolll just said, 'We're out of the car business.'"

In fact, there were other hang-ups to future Shelby production. As with the last Shelby Mustangs, some of the Shelby Dodges didn't exactly fly off the dealers' lots when new. Two things worked against the cars: they didn't carry the regular Chrysler warranty except on emissions and offered only a two year, 24,000 mile powertrain warranty. Also the late mid-year introductions meant the cars were often overlooked. By 1989, the cars had also become very expensive. As a result, Chrysler had to buy some Dakotas and CSXs back from Shelby and auction them off.

However, there were success stories. The 1986 Omni GLHS sold out quickly, due to anticipation of the first actual Shelby-produced car since 1967. Also the 1987 Charger

GLHS sold well, helped by its introduction with the other new cars. Additionally while Shelby was building his limited edition cars from 1986 to 1989 in Whittier, Chrysler was continuing to build high-profile Shelby-badged automobiles on its assembly lines. Dodge built more than 30,000 Dodge Shelby Chargers from 1983–87, plus thousands of Dodge Daytona Shelbys from 1987–91. They even produced a run of Dodge Lancer Shelbys in 1989.

Shelby Automobiles also had a hand in the early development of one of the most spectacular performance cars of the late 20th century, the Dodge Viper. Shelby Automobiles was working on a Viper chassis and turbo V-8 as early as late 1988 and early 1989. In the end, Chrysler kept the project for itself, with Carroll Shelby staying on in a consulting role.

Eventually, the parallels between what happened with Ford and the end of the Shelby Dodges were "almost textbook," Pettijohn remembered. "Carroll just doesn't play political games," he said. Also, a lot of the old regulars that were Shelby's friends at Chrysler were leaving or about to leave. It finally became much easier to just stop production and stay on with Chrysler as a performance consultant.

Truly, thirty years of American performance cars have been much the better thanks to Carroll Shelby's consultations.

INDEX

Cobra, first, 9, 10
Cobra, 1964, 14
Cobra S/C, 29
Cobra 427, 28–33
CSX-T, 1988, 82–84
coiled snake emblem, 51

Daytona Coupe, 17, 20, 21, 24
Dodge Daytona, 56
Dodge Shelby Pro Series, 91, 92

Ford GT-40, 25

GLHS Charger, 77–79
GT350, 1965, 36, 38, 69
GT350, 1970, 35
GT350, 67
GT350H, 44
GT350R, 40, 42, 43
GT500, 46, 48, 64
GT500, 1969, 64

GT500, 427-powered, 56
GT500KR, 61, 62, 63
Jones, Parnelli, 56

MacDonald, Dave, 10

Neale, Bill, 27

Omni GLHS, 76, 78

Shelby accessories, 44
Shelby Charger, 74, 75
Shelby CSX-T, 82–84
Shelby Dakota, 73, 86, 87, 89
Shelby Lancer, 73, 80
Shelby, Carroll, 90
Super Snake, 56, 58

Titus, Jerry, 56
Titus, Rick, 33
Trans-Am Mustangs, 53, 54

Viper, 90